ignore
it all
and hope
it goes
away

ignore it all and hope it goes away

poems for modern life

Nic Aubury
illustrated by Moose Allain

David Fickling Books
31 Beaumont Street
Oxford OX1 2NP, UK

ignore it all and hope it goes away – poems for modern life
is a
DAVID FICKLING BOOK

First published in Great Britain in 2022 by
David Fickling Books,
31 Beaumont Street,
Oxford, OX1 2NP

978-1-78845-156-7

1 3 5 7 9 10 8 6 4 2

Papers used by David Fickling Books are from well-managed forests and other responsible sources.

DAVID FICKLING BOOKS Reg. No. 8340307

A CIP catalogue record for this book is available from the British Library.
Printed and bound in Great Britain by Clays Ltd, Elcograf S.p.A

---

for Sophie, with thanks

contents

hello

introduction

Thank you, first of all, for picking up this book, especially if you don't normally read poetry books. I really hope you'll like this one.

The truth is, I never set out to write a poetry book. In fact, I started writing poems by mistake. From time to time ideas, jokes and observations would arrive in my head, but because I didn't have anywhere to put them, they would mostly fall out again. Then a friend of mine – who was funny and clever and knew about writing things – suggested that I should perhaps buy a notebook. So I did, and I started to put my ideas and jokes in that.

Then, one day, one of my observations turned into a short poem. It was rubbish, but I didn't especially mind, or even notice, and I decided to try to turn some more of my jokes and ideas into poems. After a while, I found that I had written quite a few of them, and that they had improved slightly. They tended to be a little bit silly – children's verse for grown-ups, more or less – and they were often quite short – partly because I am a bit lazy, but mostly because those were the sorts of poems I liked to read myself.

The poems in this book have been written over the last twelve years or so. They have been written in the corners of my life, in between well-intentioned but not always successful attempts at the everyday stuff of adulthood: being a parent, a husband, an employee, a friend, a user of technology, a reluctant attendee at parties, an increasingly soft and brittle bag of ageing and ailing humanity.

As a result, it's probably not surprising that lots of the poems are about those sorts of things – so much so that, when they were brought together into a single book, they started to feel a bit like a guide to the many and varied frustrations and absurdities of being a grown-up. It is as such that they are presented to you here – a verse companion to modern life, and all its infuriating, ridiculous, and occasionally uplifting moments.

So, if you've ever feigned interest in news about other people's children, or struggled to get out of a chair at the first attempt, or hidden in the downstairs loo from unexpected visitors, then read on . . .

Nic Aubury

friends

friends, I've often thought, are a bit like kidneys: one is plenty, no one needs more than two, and just because you've got them it doesn't mean you're eager to see them

rsvp

It seems that you like me enough that you'd ask me
to buy you a coffee machine,
some porcelainware, a patio chair,
or a Villeroy & Boch figurine;
enough that you'd ask for a Waterford vase
or a full set of white cotton bedding,
but not quite enough that you'd actually like me
to come to the whole of your wedding.

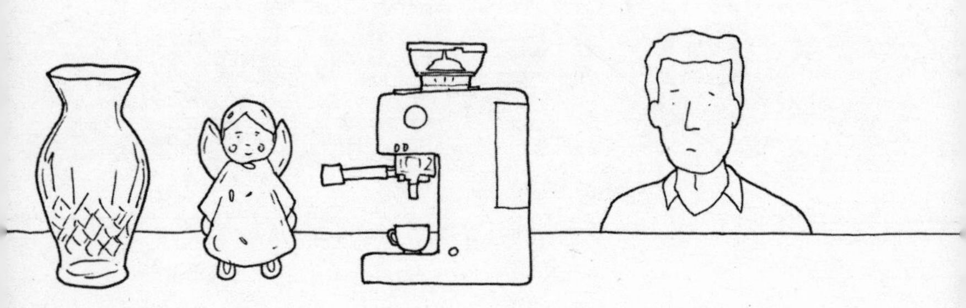

house guests

However long they stay,
however much they peeve,
they do, I'm pleased to say,
invariably leave.

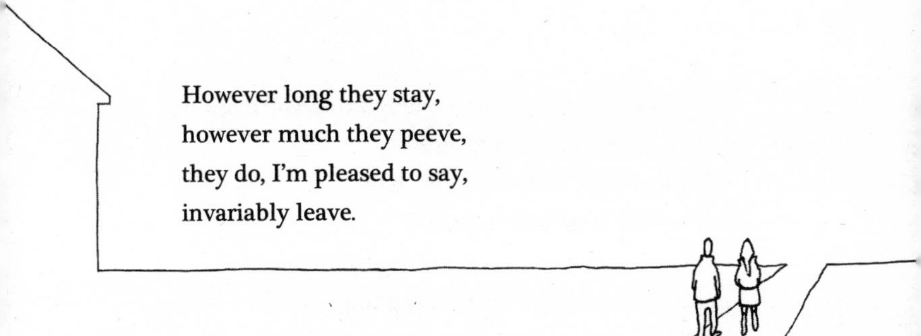

mum's the word

When you're asked to keep a secret
then it's pretty much accepted,
if you've only told one person,
that you've absolutely kept it.

ode to joy

The pleasure of one's own success
could never quite transcend
that higher form of happiness:
the failure of a friend.

bad fun

I'll gladly sign up for a toothache or flu,
or stare for an hour at the midsummer sun,
then hop for a mile with a stone in my shoe,
but spare me the torment of organised fun.

I'd rather eat handfuls of pottery shards,
all garnished with hornets, than face the distress
of pub karaoke or games of charades
or stag dos or quiz nights or themed fancy dress.

I'd tackle a Hydra, steal Geryon's herds,
or journey with Charon on Stygian streams,
in preference to hearing the blood-chilling words:
'Now everyone needs to divide into teams.'

I haven't learned much in my life, I'll admit,
but one thing I know is that fun, like a sneeze,
just happens, unbidden, is nice, then that's it;
it can't be coerced into endless reprise.

It shouldn't be scheduled or choreographed
or compèred, so give me a table for one
then leave me in peace by the door in a draught
and spare me – oh, spare me! – your organised fun.

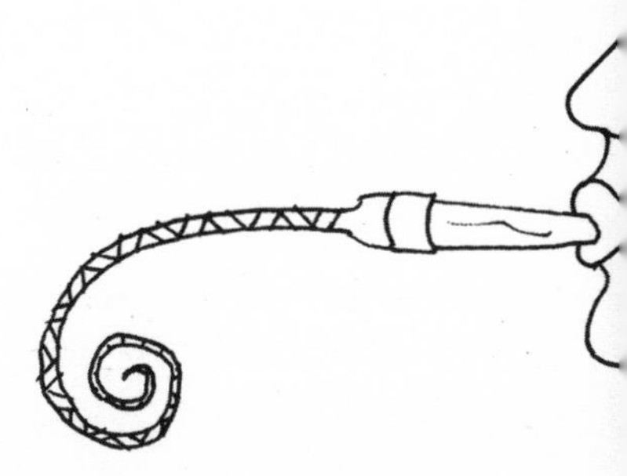

the tangled web pantoum

I told a timid little lie,
so small that it was almost true –
a dinner-party alibi –
but, once released, it fed and grew.

So small that it was almost true,
it didn't venture far at first,
but, once released, it fed and grew;
it found its voice. It spoke – conversed.

It didn't venture far at first
and then – imagine my surprise –
it found its voice; it spoke, conversed,
and soon gave birth to other lies.

And then – imagine my surprise! –
those lies all found their voices too
and soon gave birth to other lies –
much bigger ones, and not so true.

Those lies all found their voices too,
(and I'm to blame, without a doubt)
much bigger ones, and not so true,
entirely sure to catch me out.

And I'm to blame, without a doubt:
I told a timid little lie,
entirely sure to catch me out,
my dinner-party alibi.

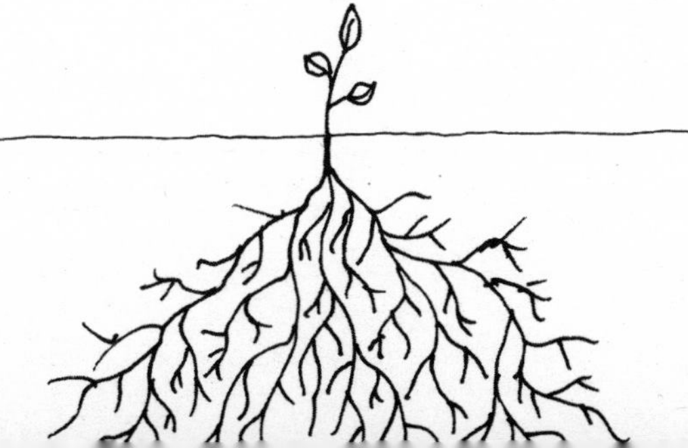

conflict resolution haiku

Your fist is raised, but
I extend an open hand –
and paper beats rock.

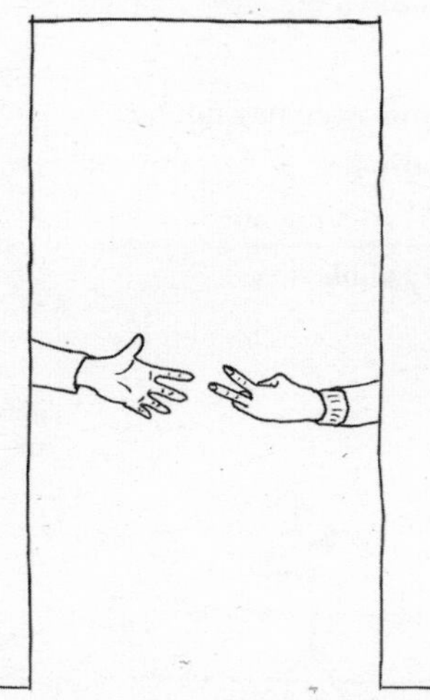

a friend indeed

You tell me when you're feeling scared
or at a loss or troubled,
and prove each time that problems shared
are really problems doubled.

the whole truth

If human beings couldn't lie
to good or wicked ends,
we'd save ourselves a lot of time
and lose a lot of friends.

costume triolet

There's only one person who likes fancy dress;
for everyone else, it just gets up their nose,
all the judging it rightly and last-minute stress.
There's only one person who likes fancy dress:
the aiming-for-witty-yet-sexy hostess
who owned just the thing for the theme that she chose.
There's only one person who likes fancy dress;
for everyone else, it just gets up their nose.

scylla and charybdis

Although I'm, as a rule, averse
to spending time with friends,
I'm also not too fond of feeling slighted;
the only kind of party worse
than one I must attend
is one to which I haven't been invited.

out to lunch

It's middle-class, English politeness
that's landed us all in this mess;
you felt that you ought to invite us,
and we felt obliged to say 'yes'.
So next time, let's say what we're thinking;
the cookbooks can stay on the shelves.
You'll save on the cost of our drinking,
and we'll get the day to ourselves.

doorbell

The only level-headed thing to do
if unexpected visitors should call
is crawl beneath their eyeline to the loo,
then lock the door and wait for night to fall.

short straw

At parties – the chatting and mingling and handing-
out-canapés sort that you have when you're older –
I've noticed how often I find myself standing
with someone more interesting over my shoulder.

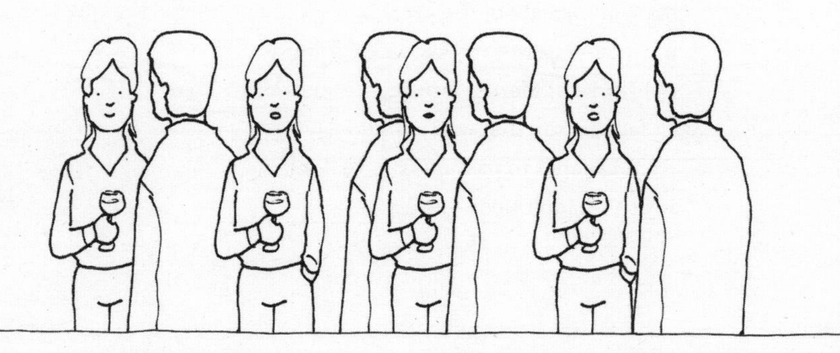

errata

I wish I hadn't said those things last night,
but after several glasses of the white
(and probably as many of the red,
if truth be told) I got it in my head
with total certainty that I was right,

and, as a consequence, I wasn't quite
as circumspect as otherwise I might
perhaps have been. Now, lying in my bed,
I wish I hadn't said

those things about the French, the Church, the plight
of wetland newts, my buttock cellulite,
the works of Marcel Proust, and sourdough bread.
In fact, I'd say that everything I said,
from canapés to passion fruit delight,
I wish I hadn't said.

work

even though we like to pretend we hate it,
work ensures we're rarely obliged to think of
other ways of filling the empty hours from
monday to friday

fyi
(an email to an employer)

For Years I've
Furthered Your Interests,
Flattering Your Investors,
Flogging Your Indemnities,
Filing Your Invoices
For You; It's
Frankly Yawn Inducing.
Finally, Yesterday I
Flipped, Yelling In
Frustration (Yet Internally,
For Yes-men Invariably
Find Yelling Imprudent):
'Fifteen Years In
Fucking Yacht Insurance!
Fifteen Years! I
Feel Yoked, Imprisoned,
Fettered! Young, Independent
Fellows Yearn Insatiably
For Youthful, Impulsive
Fun, Yet I

Follow Your Instructions
Feebly, Yield Impassively,
Feed You Information
Fawningly! Yuck! I'm
Finished Yacht Insuring!
Former Yacht Insurer,
Future Yodelling Impresario;
Flavoured Yogurt Inventor;
Farm-Yard Impersonator;
Freelance Yo-Yo Instructor!'
Following Yesterday's Incident,
Furthermore (Yikes!), I
Forwarded Your Investors
Foul, Yobbish Improprieties
From Your Inbox.
Finally – YIPPEE! – I'm
Finished Yacht Insuring.
(Freelance Yo-Yo Instructor,
For Your Information.)

summer calling

When teachers cite vocation as the reason why they chose
a life imparting knowledge to our youth,
they are, as any educator past or present knows,
a vowel away from telling you the truth.

thx & rgds

You may be important and terribly stressed,
but no one's too busy for vowels, I'd suggest.

job description

The title 'poet' comprehends
a multitude of sins,
and redefines where 'freelance' ends
and 'unemployed' begins.

from a publisher

Your book is a triumph – so clever, and such an ingenious twist at the end!
In fact, we've decided we like it so much that we want you to write it again.

start as you mean to go on

I cannot hide the joy I feel
in undertaking something new.
My starts are always full of zeal –
a cheerful will to see things through.

In undertaking something new
I rarely plan – just dive straight in.
A cheerful will to see things through
takes hold of me as I begin.

I rarely plan, just dive straight in.
Then boredom, mixed with mounting dread,
takes hold of me as I begin
to understand what lies ahead.

Then boredom, mixed with mounting dread
and waning vigour, presses me
to understand what lies ahead:
an end to my alacrity.

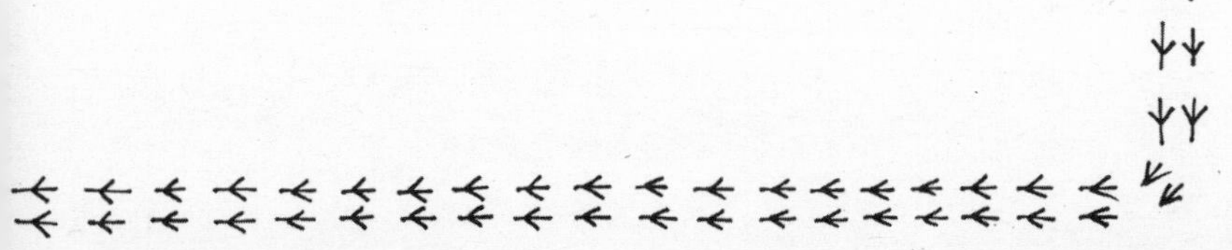

And waning vigour presses me;
the wind is taken from my sails.
An end to my alacrity;
my last enthusiasm fails.

The wind is taken from my sails
and, throwing in the towel, it's true:
my last enthusiasm fails.
I need to look for something new.

And, throwing in the towel, it's true,
I cannot hide the joy I feel.
I need to look for something new;
my starts are always full of zeal.

a cambridge limerick

A fellow of Gonville and Caius
was famously tricky to plaius.
When asked what he thought
of his students, he'd snort:
'They get worse every year by degraius.'

the wager

On balance, I would rather spend my days
in suited servitude than have to try
to think of other, more rewarding ways
of filling up the hours before I die.

mi biro es su biro

The law of theft and property,
on which our common weal depends,
we understand instinctively,
does not apply to ballpoint pens.

ambition / ambitioff

Good luck to those who chase a goal
and drive themselves to beat the rest
and scrabble up the greasy pole,
but I'll take poor and not so stressed.

love

often, when relationships stay the course, it's
less a case of happily ever after,
more that neither person can really face the
hassle of packing

the couple upstairs

Their bed springs start to creak;
their ardour has awoken.
That's twice at least this week;
their telly must be broken.

nearly over

In spite of everything, I'm pleased to say
I think I might be nearly over you.
I now at least no longer hope that true
misfortune, grief and pain might come your way,
or close my eyes in bed each night and pray
you'll suffer for the things you put me through.
No, minor inconvenience will do,
and irritating blights upon your day.
I hope your zip gets stuck, and that your sock
slips down inside your shoe a little bit.
I hope you drop your fork, and that your chair
has one uneven leg which makes it rock –
enough to leave you feeling slightly shit,
but not so much that anyone will care.

april fool

He woke on the morning of April the first
and saw his wife standing there, already dressed
in her coat, with a bag and a speech she'd rehearsed:
'I'm leaving,' she said. 'I'll come back for the rest.'
Now, seven years on, he won't call her a bitch
or resent her. He smiles; he's a reasonable bloke,
and he has to admire all the trouble to which
she has gone for the sake of a practical joke.

relationship maths

Ninety-nine per cent
faithful equals one hundred
per cent unfaithful.

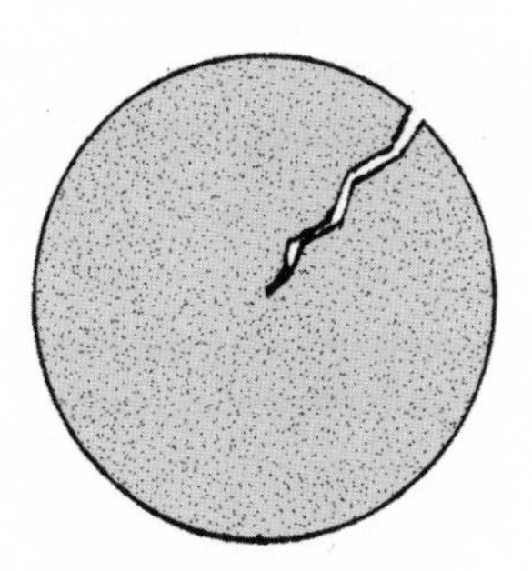

yesterlove

About a dozen years ago, you wrote
our names in biro underneath the Queen
along the bottom of a ten-pound note
I'd taken from the NatWest cash machine
near Boots. We spent it in the Old Nag's Head
on rum and Coke for you and beer for me
and, as we drank it on its way, you said
one day we'd get it back; we'd probably
be married, and we'd show our kids and laugh
about the past. And every time I get
a tenner, even now, I pause for half
a second just to check it, and regret,
while folding it behind my actual wife
and kids, that once-imagined, unlived life.

home truth

However close to feminine
perfection she might come,
it's hard to love a girl who shares
a first name with your mum.

the spur

His wife read a thing, which some therapist wrote,
that said having a lot of spontaneous sex
was the secret to keeping your marriage afloat,
so they've pencilled some in for the week after next.

monopoly haiku

She wanted to be
the dog. I'm always the dog.
I gave her the boot.

marry-go-round

We've stayed together more than half our lives, and through it all,
whatever little trials have come our way,
we've only had one argument, as far as I recall –
it's just we've had it several times a day.

misconception

If ever they should stop to think it through,
the fact of their existence might perplex
the callow youths who seem to hold the view
unshakeably that they invented sex.

the level

Relationships need honesty
and trust if they're to last – that's why
I want you to be straight with me
(unless it's bad, in which case, lie).

courting

In private, men would all admit
to thinking that in lieu
of dashing looks or charm or wit,
tenacity will do.

a rogue by any other name

A Xavier would not have been so bad.
A Dario, a Serge, a Jean-Pierre,
a Sven, an Alessandro or a Vlad
would all have been much easier to bear.
You left me for a man called Martin, though,
which (whilst it might be easy to pronounce)
does not suggest a chisel-featured beau
so much as someone working in accounts.
And, after you had told me, I was less
affected by your loss than by the shame
of playing second fiddle, I confess,
to someone with a slightly rubbish name.
And now my only solace is to pray
he'll leave you for a Marjorie one day.

on wooing

Correcting her grammar
will rarely enamour.

having kids

some have said that children are quite like farts: our own are fine – and even a source of certain pride – but other people's are almost always pretty revolting

(n-1)

The mother of five reckons four was a breeze
while the mother of four dreams of what she could do
as a mother of three (who would manage with ease,
so she says, if she'd stayed as a mother of two).
And the mother of two thinks the mother of one
has the easiest time while bemoaning her lot,
for the number of children you need to have fun
is exactly one less than the number you've got.

calling home

'Oh, hello, Dad. I've got some news:
she packed her bags today and left;
the book's been getting great reviews;
your grandson's just been done for theft;
I found a hoard of Roman gold
while digging out the flower bed;
a Russian drug cartel, I'm told,
has put a bounty on my head.'
I've tried excitement, nonchalance,
and variations thereupon;
there's only ever one response:
'Oh, right. I'll put your mother on.'

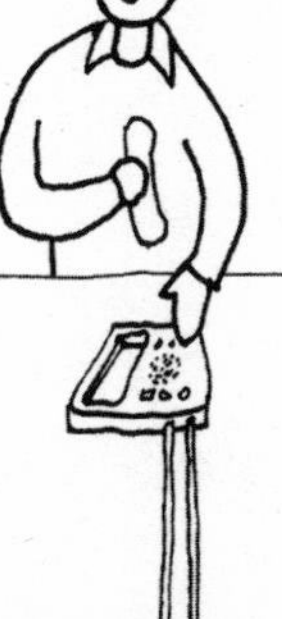

scion

A parent's love is wholly pure,
unfathomably deep,
and hardly ever felt before
their kids have gone to sleep.

other people's children

Harry, we're told, is prodigiously bright.
Harry's viola is such a delight.
Harry learns Spanish and Harry plays chess.
Of course, Harry's bedroom is never a mess.
Harry read Dickens before he was ten.
Harry's the victor ludorum – again.
Whatever he tries, Harry's marvellous at,
but everyone else thinks that Harry's a twat.

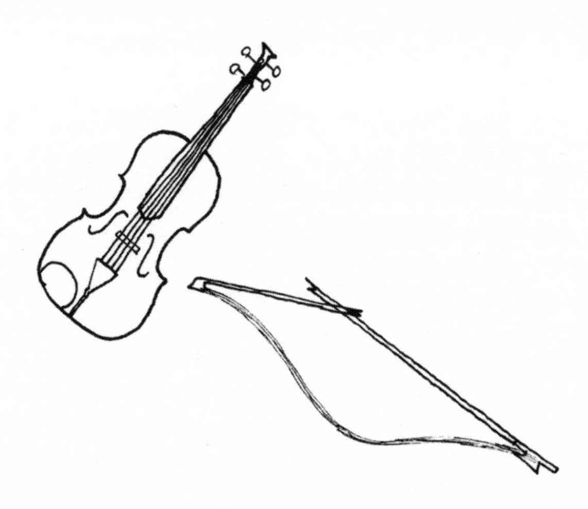

idyll

Enchanted days of scrambling over dunes
and flying homemade kites on windswept fens,
or never-ending summer afternoons
of muddy-shoed adventuring with friends
– of rope swings over streams and tree-house dens –

are well and good, but childhoods need their share
of moping aimlessly, and getting dragged
around the shops; of thinking life's unfair
whenever a reproachful finger's wagged;
of chores and clearing up and being nagged;

of arguments and feelings of profound
embarrassment. The child who's not resigned
to life's inequities, whose days abound
with joy and happiness, will be, you'll find,
too sad or scared to leave it all behind.

child of our times

Monday's child is on her phone.
Tuesday's child would like a loan.
Wednesday's child is underdressed.
Thursday's child is so, like, stressed.
Friday's child likes gaming and tweeting.
Saturday's child has issues with eating,
and the child who's born on the Sabbath day
is not a fucking kid, okay?

just desserts

Having siblings teaches you
from fifty yards to figure
which piece of chocolate cake of two
is very slightly bigger.

karma for parents

The universe, in all its boundless wonder, awe and dread,
repays us (I have lately understood)
for childhoods spent complaining that we had to go to bed
with adulthoods spent wishing that we could.

moral relatives

The rule my sons have always had,
as far as I'm aware,
is: being good's just being bad
when Mummy isn't there.

brooding

By chance, or our maker's sadistic design,
the parenthood years are a one-for-one blend
of reasons to wish them away at the time
and reasons to long for them back when they end.

school report translator

An ever-lively presence in this set,
your son contributes frequently in class
(among the things he hasn't mastered yet
are shutting up and sitting on his arse).
His written work's improved throughout the year
(it couldn't very well have got much worse)
and lately he has found a higher gear
(though bear in mind he started in reverse).
He's at his best researching things online
(he plagiarised some work, which wasn't bad).
As long as he revises, he'll do fine
(and if my mum had balls, she'd be my dad).
I'm sure next year we'll see him start to bloom
(who cares? He'll be in someone else's room).

adulting

once you've got to parenting age yourself, you can't help feeling sorry for all the kids who look towards the adults and just assume we know what we're doing

an imposter's guide to adulthood

Until you know for sure they're on to you,
or someone points and shouts: 'That man's a fraud!'
just copy what the proper grown-ups do.

Work fifty weeks a year to pay for two
pretending to enjoy yourself abroad.
Until you know for sure they're on to you,

you ought to try to give your point of view
when asked for it, and not get overawed.
Just copy what the proper grown-ups do,

and try to learn the art of sitting through
an evening out and not appearing bored;
until you know for sure they're on to you,

you can't admit you haven't got a clue
which fork to use or when you should applaud:
just copy what the proper grown-ups do.

It's possible, in fact, to muddle through
for years on end, unnoticed or ignored:
until you know for sure they're on to you,
just copy what the proper grown-ups do.

an imposter's guide: postscript

Whenever you feel like a fraud, and you fret that the genuine grown-ups can probably tell that you're making it up as you go, don't forget that everyone else is pretending as well.

the sommelier and some liar

Knowledgeable-nonchalant,
I tell the waiter: 'Fine,'
when really what I'm thinking is:
'I'm fairly sure it's wine.'

the lesson

My youth was spent embarrassed and concerned
by what the world might think, as I recall.
Then adulthood began the day I learned
the world would barely think of me at all.

moveable feast

I wonder what initially inspired
those people, whom the rest of us should thank
for finding out that tastes could be acquired,
to keep on eating food they thought was rank.

what i've learned

for Tom and Jamie

When choosing from life's biscuit tin
you'll find, on most occasions,
that what you took for chocolate chips
are sadly only raisins.

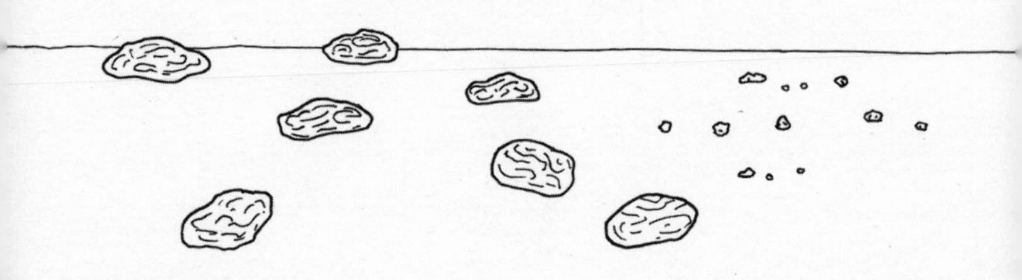

two jars

You know where you are with
both joy and despair;
it's the not knowing which
I find harder to bear.

first hamlet clerihew

Polonius,
whose counsel I consider entirely erroneous,
should have told his son that the debtor
enjoys life better.

staples

Unless you're in the market for some wider fitting shoes,
an Ayurvedic spa weekend to help yourself relax,
an awning for the patio, a Nordic river cruise,
a stair-lift, a conservatory, elasticated slacks,
a Cornish cottage mini-break for five to seven guests,
a special issue coin to mark some milestone of the Queen's,
a walk-in bath, a sofa, or a pair of bigger breasts,
you needn't read beyond halfway in glossy magazines.

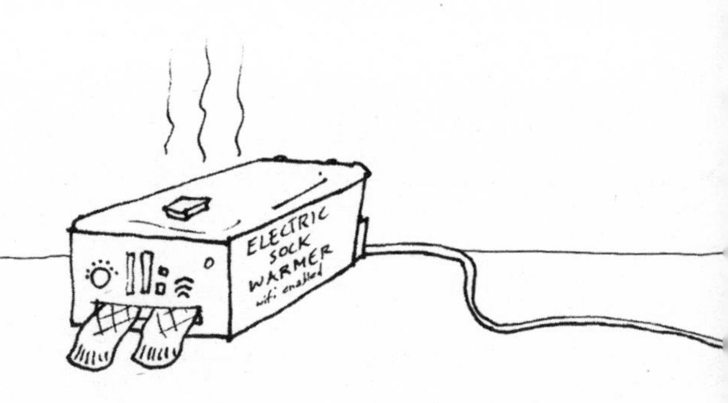

(al)truism

'By putting other people first
you'll find you always do what's best,'
is wisdom that is oft-rehearsed
by other people, I'd suggest.

unfinished symphony

I've come to learn it doesn't pay to chase
your dreams too hard: fulfilment is, I find,
in every instance smaller than the space
anticipation of it leaves behind.

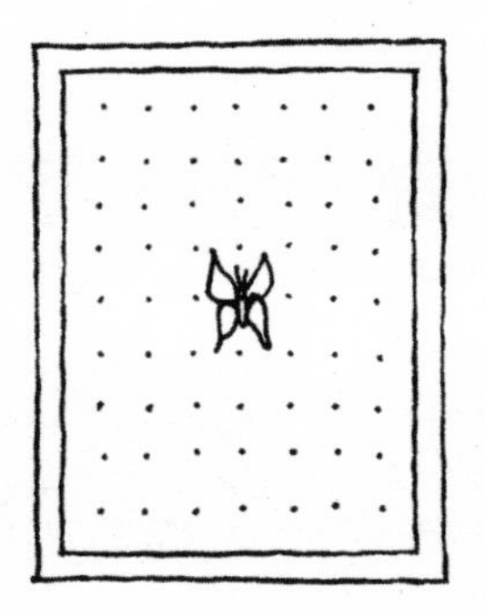

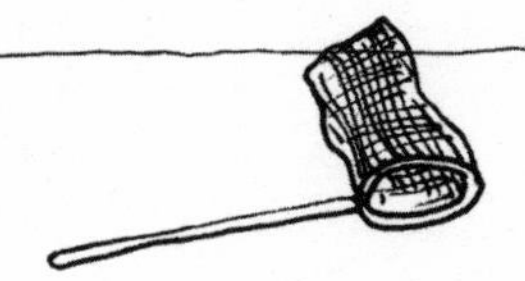

unfairy tale

I wish I could console you with the hope of happy endings
or of swift poetic justice, or unlikely strokes of luck.
I fear, though, that the truth is, if you're born an ugly duckling,
then there's every chance, in time, that you'll become an ugly duck.

self help

You ought to make a list of things to do
in order of importance every day,
then, once you've typed it up and checked it through,
ignore it all and hope it goes away.

holidays

after all that planning and preparation,
not to mention spending a modest fortune,
no one seems to want to admit to feeling
glad when it's over

the visitors' book

The Rileys said they had a super time,
the Hendersons were sad they had to leave,
and everything was utterly sublime,
I'm pleased to say, for Annabel and Steve.
Just us then, it would seem, who had a week
of bickering and sheltering inside
while moods and weather both became more bleak.
'We've had a really lovely stay,' I lied.

crossing

There isn't, to my knowledge, any law
prohibiting the trafficking of socks
and unwashed pants; I'm also fairly sure
that border guards at Britain's major docks
aren't clamping down on duck-shaped rubber rings.
I can't remember seeing on the news
reports of orchestrated customs stings
on families importing canvas shoes
and plastic tennis sets, still caked with sand.
And in my heart of hearts, of course, I know
that travel sickness pills aren't contraband
narcotics. But I find that, even so,
there's still a little frisson in the air
when driving back through 'Nothing to Declare'.

summer jam

The freedom of the open road
imparts a special joy, I'd say,
when, nose-to-tail, the cars have slowed
to crawling pace the other way.

the threshold

I turn the key and force the door across
a sliding welcome mat of junk and bills,
the evening sunlight dazzling on the gloss
of skirting boards and dusty window sills.
A fortnight's worth of trattoria plates,
and linen-shirted strolls, and local wine,
and novels by the pool, evaporates
as all I see is gloriously mine.
Tomorrow, I must go and fetch the cat,
and mow the lawn, and hang the washing out.
For now, though – well, to hell with all of that.
My favourite chair confirms beyond all doubt,
whatever one professes when in Rome,
that travel's greatest joy is coming home.

solstice

The joy of summer's longest day
is somewhat tempered every year
when, wearily, you sigh and say:
'Oh well – it's all downhill from here.'

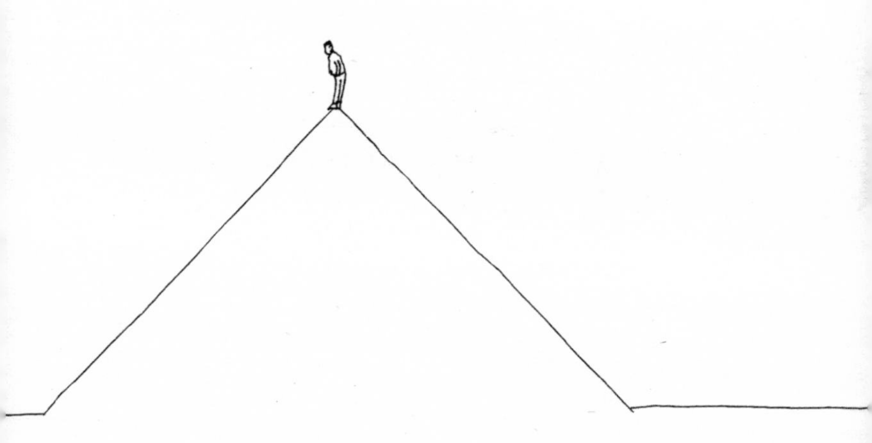

haiku for equinox

Not what you get when
you cross a horse with a cow,
disappointingly.

trick or treat

'Just give us what we want, you jerk,
or else!' It's more or less
the way the Kray twins used to work,
but done in fancy dress.

november haiku

That smell of wood-smoke,
so redolent of autumn . . .
Shit. The shed's on fire.

christmas circular

Dear friends, another year has passed
and whilst we'd love to gloat
this family has, first to last,
done bugger all of note.

gift-tag haiku

If you don't unwrap
this, then it's socks *and* a book.
Love from Schrödinger.

progress

human beings, after inventing lots of
labour-saving tools in pursuit of leisure,
then invented boredom and stress to fill the
days that they'd emptied

page not found

Now, pay attention, children, please;
it's not too tricky. Look:
if something starts with 'Mac-' or 'Face-'
it's not an actual book.

let's call the whole thing odd*

I say 'suave' and you say 'state';
I say 'digit', you say 'eight';
I say 'soak' and you say 'rock';
I say 'coal' and you say 'cock';
I say 'stop' and you say 'rump';
I say 'runs' and you say 'pump';
I say 'jazz' and you say 'lazy';
I say 'fairy', you say 'daisy'.
I say 'bald', and you say 'cake';
I say 'calf', and you say 'bake';
at first I was a bit perplexed;
I've now switched off predictive text.

* in loving memory of the Nokia 3310 – gone but not forgotten

XXX

Written to mark the 30th anniversary of the World Wide Web

The sum of all the Posts and Tweets and Comments there have been
since nineteen eighty-nine has categorically dispelled
the notion that there might be some relationship between
the truth of our opinions and the zeal with which they're held.

benchmark

The world has seen the internet,
the hovercraft, the hybrid car,
the satellite, the jumbo jet,
the Slinky and the Wonderbra,
the microchip, the mobile phone,
the female contraceptive pill,
the Rubik's Cube, the ovine clone,
the laser and the bar-code till,
the microwave, the pre-shrunk jean,
the ballpoint pen, the Post-it Note,
the automated cash machine,
the television set remote,
the training shoe, the online date,
the horizontal airline bed,
and all since nineteen twenty-eight
when someone thought of slicing bread.

o, tempora!

These venal and divided times, this age which has forsworn
all decency and reason, will, however strange it seems,
in time become a nobler past to people not yet born,
as once it was to those long dead a future full of dreams.

in loco

× Unsent Tweets

My kids are always staring at a screen;
I'm sure it must affect their mental health.
I sometimes think I ought to intervene –
but then I'd have to bring them up myself.

○ Everyone can reply

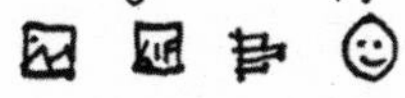

Tweet

3000 AD

In years to come, if future archaeologists should find
these settlements of ours, I wonder what they might suggest
the mystical significance or purpose was behind
the plastic bag of other plastic bags we all possessed.

wellness

science shows that doing a hundred sit-ups
every day, then drinking a spinach smoothie
helps you live much longer, but leaves you wishing
death would come sooner

the salad drawer

The fridge has got a special drawer
for keeping fruit and salad in;
it's less a storage box and more
an air-conditioned compost bin
where bags of leaves can putrefy
in fetid liquid by themselves
and leave unsullied all the pie
and cheesecake on the other shelves.

midnight rumbler

for Phoebe Jones

If snacks aren't meant for eating in the middle of the night,
then tell me why the fridge has got that helpful little light.

feeder

A fry-up, then elevenses,
a Sunday roast, then tea.
By god, she puts the 'hospital'
in 'hospitality'.

consternutation

There isn't an ointment
or salve that can ease
the cruel disappointment
of losing a sneeze.

sick note

The world does not accept the fact –
I fear it never will –
that even hypochondriacs
are sometimes really ill.

pear-shaped

I've given up on dieting
for good, as, on the whole,
self-loathing's so much easier
to do than self-control.

21st-century logic

I'm overweight; I must get slim.
I drive a mile to join the gym.
I run two treadmill miles and then
I drive a mile back home again.

purveyors of the finest

You never see crests
claiming royal appointment
on pregnancy tests
or on haemorrhoid ointment.

face value

When people say: *You're looking well,*
I wish that they'd elaborate.
I always find it hard to tell,
when people say: *You're looking well,*
if what they mean is: *Bloody hell,*
you're hot! or: *Wow! You've put on weight!*
or even just: *You're looking well.*
I wish that they'd elaborate.

the jaffa cake paradox

I've eaten far too many; I should stop.
I'd have to stop if all of them were gone.
They would be gone if someone ate them up.
So, actually, I ought to carry on.

nature

all those David Attenborough things in childhood helped me understand that the natural world, in all its fragile wonder, is best enjoyed by watching the telly

bertrand russell's chicken

'The man who has fed the chicken every day throughout its life at last wrings its neck instead, showing that more refined views as to the uniformity of nature would have been useful to the chicken.'

(Bertrand Russell, The Problems of Philosophy.
Reproduced with permission of the Licensor through PLSclear.)

Each morning, he would cross the little yard
which lay between the farmhouse and our shed,
and every day, the same slow, heavy tread
of thick-soled work boots scuffing on the hard
brick path would let us know we'd soon be fed.

Then, chirping a falsetto 'Chook, chook, chook!'
he'd open wide the makeshift henhouse door,
which scarred concentric arcs across the floor,
and scatter corn. It fell in every nook
and cranny – nestled down among the straw.

So how could we have known what he would do –
so quickly, too, before we'd understood
quite what was happening? No – no one could.
The man that day was not the one we knew –
a simple husbandman whose heart was good.

He hasn't ever been that way again,
and things are back exactly as they were –
except, of course, we all remember her.
And every day we hear his boots, and then
the door, the scattered corn, the others stir.

finale

We shouldn't look at butterflies
and pity them their plight,
although they only live a little while,
but rather see our summer skies
as teeming with a flight
of caterpillars going out in style.

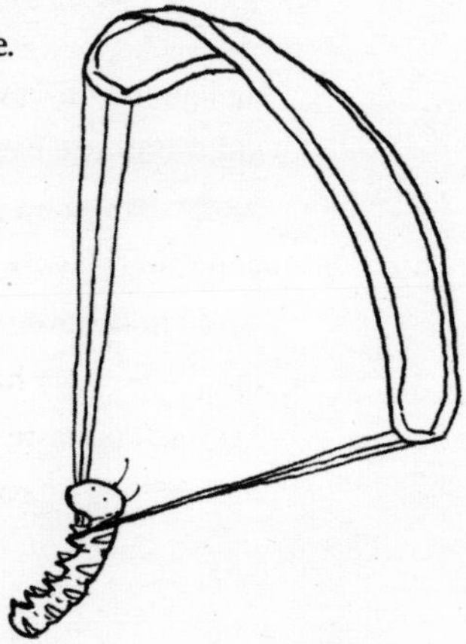

love bites

Could anyone of sound and sober mind,
appraising our respective strengths and flaws,
regard us lying side by side and find
my body more desirable than yours?
Who wouldn't gaze with wonderment upon
your smoothly sculpted back and slender thighs,
or, equally, not look at mine, all wan
and plump, and quickly turn away their eyes?
You'd stir the most recalcitrant of loins;
your ankles, wrists and neck are turned with grace,
while mine are just the fleshy bits which join
my body to my hands and feet and face.
Yet, lacking taste or bloody-mindedly,
mosquitoes fly past you to feast on me.

birdsong

The chorus which you've doubtless always heard
as giving voice to nature's harmony
in fact, translated literally from Bird,
means: 'Oi, you little tit – you're in my tree.'

reflection on the water

for Kathleen Geere

The sea would be greatly improved, there's no doubt,
if they took all the creatures with razor-toothed smiles
and suckers and stingers and tentacles out,
then filled it with chlorine and lined it with tiles.

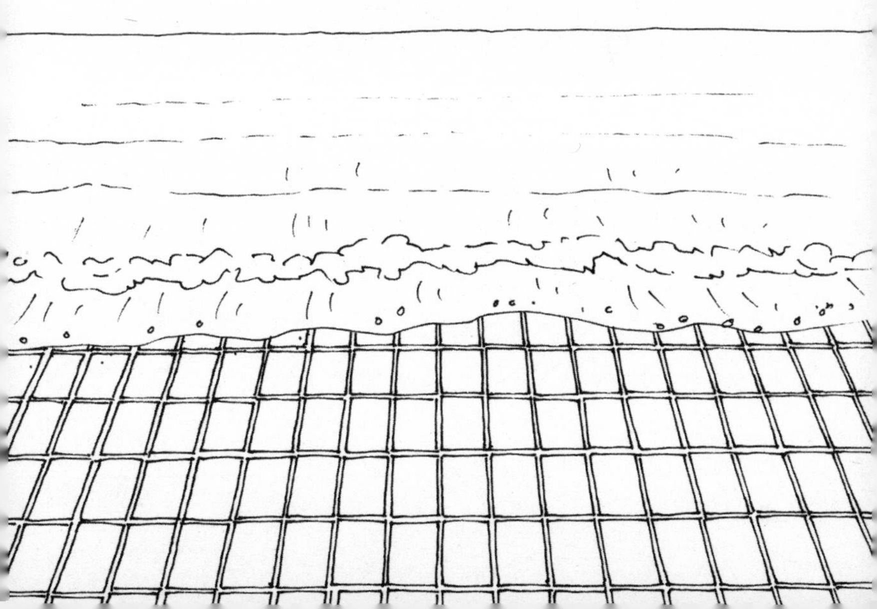

window pain

I've stopped again; I don't know why:
there's nothing there that I can see.
Perhaps I'll just have one more try,

except, this time, I think I'll fly
a bit more single-mindedly.
I've stopped again. I don't know why

a sudden patch of solid sky
keeps popping up in front of me.
Perhaps I'll just have one more try;

I've always thought, by aiming high,
you end up where you want to be.
I've stopped again; I don't know why.

I think I've bruised my compound eye
and bent my wing irreparably.
Perhaps I'll just have one more try –

I'm really not the sort of guy
who gets put off that easily.
I've stopped again; I don't know why.
Perhaps I'll just have one more try.

eco worrier

Oh, let's not abandon the Earth to its fate
while rainforests burn and the polar ice melts!
We ought to take action before it's too late
– and clearly by 'we' I mean 'everyone else'.

magpie smallprint

One for sorrow, two for joy,
three for a girl, four for a boy,
five for silver, six for gold,
*seven for a secret never to be told**

*But just how close in time and space do magpies need to be
for them to count on aggregate and not just separately?
If I should see one magpie now, and then one more tomorrow,
would that be two for joy, or just a double dose of sorrow?
And what if you get eight or more at once? It may be rare,
but is the whole thing then just void? That doesn't seem quite fair.
And can you split them into groups? If I saw seven, say,
I'd rather joy plus silver than a secret any day.
With stuff like joy and sorrow the distinction is important,
and as things stand we might expect an outcome which we oughtn't.
For matters of such magnitude, I think it's only right
to do away with shades of grey: it should be black and white.

religion/ politics

thinking other people should see the light and all at once agree with our views is still the most effective way to begin a war, or ruin a friendship

letters spray

'Suggesting that the universe could have been created by a "big bang" is like suggesting that the Bible could have been created by an explosion in a printing press.'
(Argument offered by a creationist in support of the idea of intelligent design.)

ass arse save ear tortoise
sew letters spray:
half arthur
hoo heart inn evan
hallo bee fine aim
thigh king dumb calm
thigh wilbur dun
unearth our settees inn evan
gear vase the stay hard hailey bred
anne four give ass art rest passes
ass weaver give though suit rest pass again stars
lee dust nut enter temp station
butt dear liver russ farm eve all
four vine beaver kin dumb
kerpow! her anther chlorine
far river endeavour
our men

creation theory

Whoever thought a baby's head
would fit through a vagina
does not deserve the epithet
'intelligent designer'.

saints and saints' abilities

(which may or may not be sung to the tune of
Monty Python's 'Galaxy Song')

St Matthew must have beaten lots of Matthews to the role,
surpassing them in faith and moral worth,
and think of what a mark you'd have to make to top the poll
of all the good and pious Marks on Earth.
It's safe-ish to assume the field was similarly big
when heaven was appointing a St Paul;
I cannot, though, imagine that, for him to land the gig,
St Pancras had to do that much at all.

Imagine all the effort that St Andrew and St James
put in to get themselves beatified,
when others who were lucky to have more unusual names
were canonised but barely even tried:
I reckon that, to get their jobs, a single goodish deed
was ample for St Swithin and St Ive,
and, after he'd been christened, that St Neot didn't need
to do much more than simply stay alive.

They say you need to strive if you're determined to succeed,
but, if you're not the striving sort, take heart:
a lack of competition means success is guaranteed
with very little effort on your part,
and any loving parents, who, with all due reverence, claim
celestial ambitions for their heirs,
should simply call them something that is not in fact a name,
and, rest assured, the job's as good as theirs.

spoiled ballot

I couldn't vote for anyone
who, by his own volition,
with all the jobs he could have done,
became a politician.

the problem

Whatever his position,
a man's array of talents
and level of ambition
so rarely seem to balance.

impasse

We need to find a compromise,
and, honestly, I think we might
if everybody really tries
their hardest to accept I'm right.

idiotville

We like the opinions we've already got,
so why should we want to exchange them for yours?
We're not too concerned if they're valid or not;
we like the opinions we've already got
and find, if we say them and tweet them a lot,
they're greeted with our-sort-of-people's applause.
We like the opinions we've already got,
so why should we want to exchange them for yours?

ageing

once or twice a year at the most for one, and several times a week for the other: slowly, as we age, our timetables switch for sex and doctors' appointments

good gran / bad gran

Good Gran had dimples and hair in a bun;
Bad Gran had gout and a whiskery beard.
Good Gran told stories and loved having fun;
Bad Gran was grumpy and smelled a bit weird.
Good Gran made biscuits and flapjacks and treats;
Bad Gran made liver and onions with mash.
Good Gran gave fifty-pence pieces for sweets;
Bad Gran had tins, which she hid, full of cash.
Good Gran had cupboards of marbles and games;
Bad Gran had varicose veins and a cough.
Good Gran had goldfish with humorous names;
Bad Gran drank sherry, and then nodded off.
Good Gran had hats topped with tropical fruits;
Bad Gran had nets that she wore on her head.
Good Gran was caught nicking lipstick from Boots;
'It's never the ones you'd expect,' Bad Gran said.

descent of man

In youth, before I knew the cares
of middle age, I never dreamt
that getting out of comfy chairs
could take me more than one attempt.

v-necks from the flames

It's cyclical, which clothes are in
and which are out of style;
let others be the judge of whether I'm
a man who simply hasn't been
out shopping for a while
or a fashion icon, years before his time.

the daily grind

'Routine in an intelligent man is a sign of ambition' (W.H. Auden)

The sort of track that livestock wear
across a grassy ridge
has formed between my telly chair,
the toilet and the fridge.

night run

With age you have to learn the knack
(or else forgo your bedside cup)
of getting to the loo and back
before you've fully woken up.

the hunter-gatherer

I zigzag slowly through the aisles
of packets, tins and ready meals,
past staff with here-to-help-you smiles
and signs proclaiming discount deals,
and while I'm weighing up my choice
between some different tinned sardines,
from deep within, an ancient voice
cries out: 'This can't be what it means
to be a man!' I turn, and then
a sudden notion fills my mind
to join my fellow shopping men –
to run outside, to leave behind
these bright, refrigerated shelves,
where all our needs and wants are piled,
and hunt for canapés ourselves
and gather loo rolls in the wild.

de senectute

My body is a temple, but
it's one like Rome's or Greece's:
a hundred generations old,
and fallen half to pieces.

the cycling club

Those men in their forties in tight-fitting shorts
disprove what they say about pint-pots and quarts.

reflections on piaf

What, *honestly*, Edith? *Rien de rien?*
No hint of remorse, or the slightest chagrin?
I'm pleased for you, truly, but faintly surprised:
my regrets are in volumes, and alphabetised.

retired

When all you have to do each day
is watch a neighbour mow his lawn
and feed the cat, it's cruel, I'd say,
of life to wake you up at dawn.

the english

anyone who's normally half-embarrassed, half-apologetic, but still retains a nagging sense they ought to be put in charge, is probably English

page 155

rhyme nor reason

You can't rhyme 'plough' with 'cough' or 'rough',
or 'thorough', 'through' or 'though';
hough foreigners can learn this stough
I troughly wouldn't knough.

decline and fall

(A cautionary tale, which may or may not be sung to the tune of Gilbert & Sullivan's 'Major-General's song')

When Homer wrote the *Iliad* and latterly the *Odyssey*
(one heroey-and-battley, one monstery-and-goddessy)
he put in verse some fundamental lessons for humanity –
and way before those Bible guys invented Christianity.
Then Homer was the model for the epic of Vergilius
(or Virgil as we call him now, to sound less supercilious).
For centuries, our scholars read his masterful hexameters
but nowadays they fall outside curricular parameters.
And so it is with Plato, and with Greece's great tragedians:
our schools are far too busy teaching means and modes and medians,
and coding, and the features of Galapagoan tortoises
to bother with them any more, or Ovid's *Metamorphoses*.
Instead of reading Cicero's sublime, forensic oratory
our children learn what colour something turns in a laboratory
when something else is added, and their teachers all consider these
experiments, who oughtn't, more important than Thucydides.
For pedagogues today, equating relevance with recency,
have shunned our ancient texts without propriety or decency
resulting in our cultural and moral disinheritance,
which means we're now no better than the – OMG! – Americans.

neither barrel

A tut is the click that an Englishman makes
when, affronted, he's quick to react
and he fires a rebuke, but discovers too late
that his mouth wasn't loaded, in fact.

horse-posh

They march around the countryside and find each other funny;
they dress the same and all have names like Dinky, Fizz and Bunny;
they speak in streams of barely comprehensible elision;
they're basically the Teletubbies' cavalry division.

horror show

No English phrase
can stir a sense
of panic in a man
in quite the ways
that 'audience
participation' can.

twin town

Your Gallic name beneath our sign
feels chic to us, it's true,
but maybe 'Chipping Sodbury' sounds
quite glamorous to you.

ode to spring

The English spend May putting outfits together
which would have been perfect for yesterday's weather.

honesty

By a low cottage wall that was bordered with phlox
on an old garden table with rickety legs
was some produce for sale, and an honesty box,
so I posted a note: 'I have stolen your eggs'.

expertese

My accent when I'm talking to
a builder or mechanic
turns slightly more malt vinegar
and slightly less balsamic.

glove song

Walking near the park on an autumn evening
someone kind, I notice, has left a single
glove they've found pulled over a fleur-de-lis on
top of the railings,
puddle-damp, but holding its fingers upwards,
waving bravely, hoping a passer-by might
reunite it joyfully with its aran,
cable-knit soulmate.
First-day schoolboys, nervously glancing backwards,
wave like that while trying to swallow down that
special kind of throat-gripping sadness saved for
just such occasions.
No one's coming back for that glove; they might have
even bought a new pair already, blithely
unaware that somewhere the one they've lost is
waving and hoping.

the end

life, for all its manifold irritations,
still provides a passably entertaining
way to pass the time in the slowly snaking
queue for the graveyard

(1974–   )

I'm waiting for a second date
to balance out my brackets' scales.
A living writer can't be great;
I'm waiting for a second date
to lend my reputation weight
and, hopefully, to boost my sales.
I'm waiting for a second date
to balance out my brackets' scales.

ending up

Though paradise may not exist,
I'll feel I've somehow won
if, when I die, I leave a list
of jobs I haven't done.

the thinker

The thinker used to contemplate
with scarcely any intermission
man's unhappy, mortal state,
impermanence and doomed condition.
Morbid thoughts preoccupied
his mind until his mood was such
he just gave up one day and died.
It's better not to think too much.

epitaph

I would ask, if I may,
that they carve on my tomb
what the rest of you say
when I've walked from the room.

memorial bench

Up close, I spot the tarnished little plaque,
engraved *In loving memory of Clive*
who loved this spot. Subtracting date from date –
they're etched above the greying, slatted back
as well – I pause and quickly calculate
how old he was. 'Gosh. Only fifty-five.

That really isn't any kind of age,'
I mutter as a pair of walkers pass.
My pity for his poor, imagined wife
soon fades, unlike my sense that I can gauge
my likely span from someone else's life.
I sit to eat my sandwich on the grass.

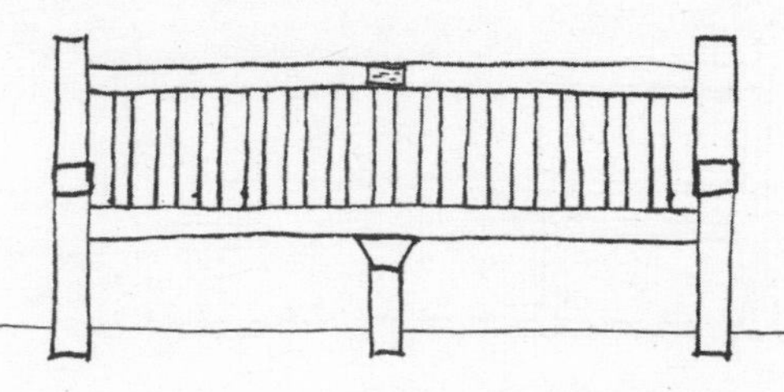

congregation

The family was there, of course, to pay
their last respects, and one or two who'd thought
on balance they should give up half a day
of annual leave to offer their support –
acquaintances and blokes he used to know
from work – came in as three began to chime.
And then, behind them, row on empty row
of things which seemed important at the time.

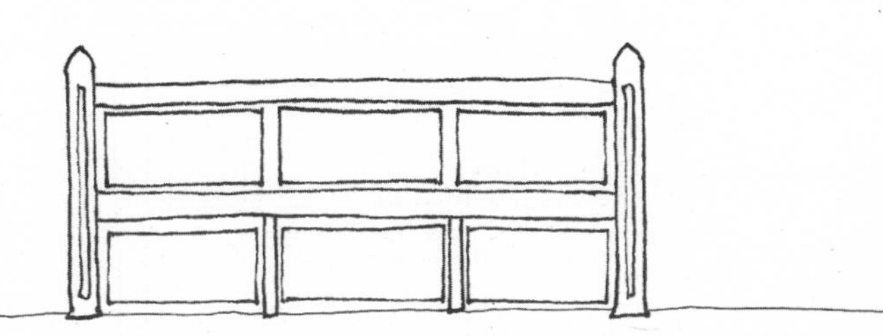

ever after

An ending can't be happy, I'm afraid.
Unless you stop the story half-way through
and slowly let the smiling picture fade,
an ending can't be happy. I'm afraid
that someone's always widowed or betrayed,
or moves away in search of pastures new.
An ending can't be happy, I'm afraid –
unless you stop the story half-way through.

being frank

And now the end is near for me,
a father, husband, employee,
and through it all, I'd have to say,
I did it someone else's way.

thanks

acknowledgements

Thanks to Luke Wright and Nasty Little Press for publishing a number of my early poems, versions of some of which are included in this volume.

Thanks to Michael Schmidt and Helen Tookey at Carcanet for including a dozen of my poems in the *New Poetries VI* anthology. A handful of those poems have also been re-written or reproduced here.

Thanks to David Fickling, Rosie Fickling, Alison Gadsby, Meggie Dennis and all at DFB for getting behind this project so wholeheartedly and enthusiastically from the start, and for the many improvements they have made so gently and tactfully along the way. They have been a joy to work with.

Thanks to the ludicrously talented Moose Allain, whose illustrations have made this book so much more fun to look at.

Thanks, especially, to Sophie Hannah, without whose generosity, wise advice and unwavering support this book would never have seen the light of day. It is dedicated to her with heartfelt gratitude.

Thanks to my lovely mum and dad for their unstinting love and support, and for sharing with me a good number of the foibles and neuroses which have given rise to these poems. Thanks, too, to my sister for always being my least objective critic and most vocal cheerleader.

Thanks, and boundless love, to Tom, Jamie, Fred and Emma, for indulging me and for enduring the ignominy of having a poet in the family.

Nic Aubury

about the author

Nic Aubury grew up in the Midlands, where he spent most of his time trying to get girls to laugh at his jokes. Then he went to university and met a girl whose jokes made him laugh. Now they have three sons, some friends they keep meaning to call, and a bag of salad rotting slowly in their fridge.

about the illustrator

Moose Allain is an artist, illustrator and dedicated tweeter who lives and works in South West England. Always on the lookout for interesting projects, his work has encompassed drawing cartoons for *Private Eye* magazine, designing murals for a beauty salon in Mexico City, co-producing the video for the band Elbow's 'Lost Worker Bee' single – he's even been tempted to try his hand at stand-up comedy. But his favourite ever job (second only to illustrating this book) was re-turfing a ha-ha while delirious with flu.